AMORGOS

NIKOS GATSOS

Amorgos

TRANSLATED BY SALLY PURCELL

WITH A PREFACE BY PETER LEVI

ANVIL PRESS POETRY

Published in 1998
by Anvil Press Poetry Ltd
Neptune House   70 Royal Hill   London   SE10 8RF
www.anvilpresspoetry.com
Reprinted in 2006

Titlepage device by Nikos Engonopoulos
made for the first edition 1943

This book is published with financial assistance
from Arts Council England

English text set in Monotype Fournier by Anvil Press Poetry
Greek text set in Times Ten Greek by Kadianakis, Athens

ISBN 0 85646 302 7

A catalogue record for this book
is available from the British Library

Publisher's Note

THIS SMALL BOOK is in some measure a memorial both to Nikos Gatsos, who died in 1992, and to Sally Purcell, who died in January 1998. Both were dedicated poets whose poetry never strayed from the path of its vision.

Sally Purcell's translation of *Amorgos* has twice appeared in limited editions: from Other Poetry Editions, Hay-on-Wye in 1980 and the Zodion Press, Athens in 1986. The only change we have made, other than to adjust minor inconsistencies in hyphenation and punctuation, is to bring the paragraphing of the translation into line with that of the Greek text.

Although the poem has allusions enough to warrant several pages of notes for non-Greek readers – and may warrant them for Greek readers too – we have printed the poem on its own. Brief notes might satisfy occasional curiosity (who Kalybas or Kolokotronis are, for example, which may easily enough be discovered) but would shed no more than the faintest flicker of light on the poem. Readers intrigued

by the poem should look at the special Gatsos issue of the annual review of modern Greek culture, *The Charioteer* (no. 36: New York, 1995–96). It has some useful essays, translations of the songs and other material of interest, which make it the best introduction to Gatsos's work that is available in English.

Sally Purcell's translation was dedicated to Peter Levi, a long-standing friend of Gatsos, about whom (among other Greek poets) he wrote memorably in *The Hill of Kronos* (1980). She made the version at his request and with some help from him, as she was rather a classical than a modern Greek scholar.

We thank Agathi Dimitrouka, Nikos Gatsos's literary executor, for her meticulous help in the preparation of this edition.

PETER JAY

POSTSCRIPT

Sadly, since the first printing of this book, Peter Levi too has died, in February 2000.

Nikos Gatsos

THE ARCADIANS, when we first hear of them, lived in remote or inaccessible fortresses. Even Homer was not at all interested in Arcadia south of its middle, but Nikos Gatsos was born at the small village covering the ruins of Aséa, which lay just north of the road between the modern centre of Arcadia, which is Tripolis, and the Hellenistic centre, which is Megalopolis (the Great City). His father was a farmer who had emigrated to America, but died on his journey out. Nikos and the family were left at Aséa with an uncle who ran the inn, which is still standing and has the dignity of one of those small buildings designed by Prince Albert in the Isle of Wight. The house where Nikos was brought up lies a few miles from the road, in the old settlement still called Aséa. It is a typical old farm house, with an external staircase leading to the front door, a row of lilies and a rough orchard garden. Near this house Nikos in his youth watched the first excavation of the ancient city of Aséa, by the Swedes in the 1930s. He is buried not far away in the same cemetery as his mother, his lame

cousin who never left home, and all his family. The old city called Aséa was one of the twelve Arcadian cities destroyed to build Megalopolis in the fourth century BC. Nikos was educated locally, but the ambitious hunger for a bigger world which has always been intense in the Greek provinces was no less so in his day. The city of Tripolis, with its Champ de Mars and its law courts, has the expansive grandeur one expects of some great nineteenth-century provincial capital.

When Nikos grew up, he went almost inevitably to Athens, where he attended the University. As a learned institution it was in most departments unimpressive, but he attended the lectures of Professor Vëis who was the most widely knowledgeable antiquarian that Greece has ever known. He would greet every new pupil with an enquiry about his local ruin or his mysterious haunted well. His publications were all pamphlets and still await (and deserve) collection. Nikos cut a dash at the University, being one of the only two students of his day to carry a walking stick. He is said to have had an affair with the daughter of one of his instructors, which ended in tears. He was apparently arrested at the request of the irate father, but for this, and for all the stories of his youth, we depend on uncertain and possibly unreliable evidence. He left the University without

a degree, and turned to making his living perhaps by gambling, and in the fifties to writing lyrics for songs on the radio. At this time he was already at work on *Amorgos*. It is not easy for a foreigner to understand how young modern Greek poetry was. The beginning of modern Greek came with the war of independence, with Solomos. In the nineteenth century the most civilized Greeks wrote charming verses like those printed by young ladies in albums in the England of Tennyson's youth. They were deadly boring and were known as the School of Athens, but only Jean Moréas, who wrote in French, and lived in Paris, was as good a poet as most minor European poets of his period. Of him I recall only the line, 'Je fume mon cigare en face des fortifications'. The big shake-up, since poetry is not after all a civilized art, came with Palamas, an intense nationalist who wrote a vast amount both in prose and in verse and lived until 1940. His views somewhat recalled William Morris and his uncontrolled output recalled either Morris or if you undervalue him then Victor Hugo, but at least his critical writings remain of great interest and he still has a strong group of supporters in the provinces. After him came Kavafis, who lived abroad, with whom modern poetry is often said to have begun. He is well enough known for me not to comment on him. The great poets of the thirties, Karyotakis and others, show how

complete the victory of modernism could be with no loss of integrity, and in George Seferis Greece had in the thirties her first seriously great poet.

Nikos Gatsos was a war-time poet. *Amorgos* is both a dated poem and I think a great one; but it is almost all that he ever wrote. It hit his generation like a thunderbolt. Amorgos is the name of a Greek island which he chose for its symbolism: it means Bitter Island, though he had never visited it and as a place it is still obscure. He was undoubtedly by this time a great master of poetry in many languages, but it was into Greek traditions, folklore and poetry of the oral tradition, that he dug to find his roots. He was as fresh as a waterfall. He used to say that if he were dictator he would make a law to prevent the Greeks learning foreign languages. His friend, contemporary and fellow poet, Elytis, was in some ways comparable: his greatest poem was the lament for the Greek Second Lieutenant lost in Albania, or perhaps *The Axion Esti*, but neither of them are quite as powerful as Gatsos, nor do they rise to the level of Dylan Thomas.

Nikos's experience during the war and the German occupation was grievous. He was called up, issued that is with a rifle and uniform, but the next day he returned them and that was the end of that. He contracted the habit of gambling in order to keep himself alive, and

gambled away what must have been a remarkable library. In those days, people gambled on the pavement in what is now central Athens. The difference between Nikos and Elytis was that Elytis was solidly middle class, rather a rarity in Greece in his generation, and had the private means to live and write, and go on writing, until he won the Nobel Prize in 1979, and took from that a new impulse which lasted until his death in 1996. His family were soap manufacturers. Nikos made nothing from his poetry however many times it was reprinted, and he added very little to his *Amorgos,* which is just one poem. His publishers did not pay, and although now a few bits and pieces have been added to his oeuvre, it is essentially just *Amorgos.* The lyrics which Nikos wrote for excellent composers and which gained him a popular reputation were published, but that edition is not complete and came at the end of his life. They were mostly written for the company Columbia which at least paid. The lyrics do not translate easily into English, although I have made some attempt in 'A Bottle in the Shade'. One must also mention that Nikos wrote a brilliantly successful version of Lorca's *Blood Wedding.* The truth is that he spent all his energies for most of his life on perfecting his lyrics, which really were lyrics, meant to be sung to music. I have heard Lorca's brother say that the Gatsos translation was as good as Lorca's text.

Seferis used to say that Gatsos was the only man whose Greek he truly envied.

As a human being Nikos was like the sweetest of grandfather elephants or the wisest and most fastidious of tortoises. He sat through afternoons in the same café at the same table for a lifetime except when the cafés shut down finally. In the sixties indeed it was possible to meet all the modern Greek poets in the Brasilian Coffee Bar in Bucharest Street on any morning but Gatsos would sit in Flocca's at the downstairs table at the back, most remote from the door. The Brasilian, all the same, was where Henry Miller met his match just before the war. He asked Gatsos and Elytis whether they liked American writers and their answer was reserved. He pressed them to know who they might have heard of. They were still reserved but at last Gatsos said, 'Elytis and I rather admire a young American writer called Henry Miller.' Henry Miller was so delighted and excited that he felt he had to go to a brothel at once to relieve his feelings. Gatsos and Elytis told him they regretted they knew nothing about such places, but they knew who could instruct him and they gave him an introduction to George Katsimbalis: that was how Henry Miller came to meet the Colossus of Maroussi. For a short time after the war, Gatsos was an assistant editor to Katsimbalis in the

Anglo-Greek Review, of which copies still occasionally turn up and are greatly prized.

His links with his home village never slackened. When he was not gambling he would spend long summer holidays there, in a large straw hat, and come back to Athens with comic stories that might have come from the depths of some province of nineteenth-century Russia. Come to think of it, his father's inn was like a Russian *khani* of 1900 and the contrast between town and country, between the big road to Tripolis and the lane that leads from behind the inn to the village, nearly deserted now, where it dies out into a track, recall an earlier period still. Along the dust of that road, white-faced and upright in a chauffeur-driven car, Nikos would travel once a week with flowers for his mother, and then drive straight back to Athens. He was interested in the minutest questions of language and dialect, and poetry never went to sleep in him. He was not like any other Athenian.

PETER LEVI

ΑΜΟΡΓΟΣ

AMORGOS

Σ' ἕνα πράσινο ἄστρο

To a green star

*Κακοὶ μάρτυρες ἀνθρώποισιν ὀφθαλμοὶ
καὶ ὦτα βαρβάρους ψυχὰς ἐχόντων.*

ΗΡΑΚΛΕΙΤΟΣ

HERACLITUS SAYS: Eyes and ears are bad witnesses to men whose souls are savage.

Diels, *Die Fragmente der Vorsokratiker*, B, 107

Μὲ τὴν πατρίδα τους δεμένη στὰ πανιὰ καὶ τὰ κουπιὰ στὸν ἄνεμο
    κρεμασμένα
Οἱ ναυαγοὶ κοιμήθηκαν ἥμεροι σὰν ἀγρίμια νεκρὰ μέσα στῶν
    σφουγγαριῶν τὰ σεντόνια
Ἀλλὰ τὰ μάτια τῶν φυκιῶν εἶναι στραμένα στὴ θάλασσα
Μήπως τοὺς ξαναφέρει ὁ νοτιὰς μὲ τὰ φρεσκοβαμένα λατίνια

Their own country is tied in their sails
    and oars hang on the wind
Shipwrecked sailors lie quiet as dead goats
    in winding-sheets of sponges
But the eyes of the seaweed
    are turned on the sea
Lest the south wind bring them home
    with new colour on their canvas

Κι ἕνας χαμένος ἐλέφαντας ἀξίζει πάντοτε πιὸ πολὺ ἀπὸ δυὸ στήθια
κοριτσιοῦ ποὺ σαλεύουν
Μόνο ν' ἀνάψουνε στὰ βουνὰ οἱ στέγες τῶν ἐρημοκκλησιῶν μὲ τὸ μεράκι
τοῦ ἀποσπερίτη
Νὰ κυματίσουνε τὰ πουλιὰ στῆς λεμονιᾶς τὰ κατάρτια
Μὲ τῆς καινούργιας περπατησιᾶς τὸ σταθερὸ ἄσπρο φύσημα
Καὶ τότε θὰ 'ρθουν ἀέρηδες σώματα κύκνων ποὺ μείνανε ἄσπιλοι
τρυφεροὶ καὶ ἀκίνητοι
Μὲς στοὺς ὁδοστρωτῆρες τῶν μαγαζιῶν μέσα στῶν λαχανόκηπων τοὺς
κυκλῶνες
Ὅταν τὰ μάτια τῶν γυναικῶν γίναν κάρβουνα κι ἔσπασαν οἱ καρδιὲς
τῶν καστανάδων
Ὅταν ὁ θερισμὸς ἐσταμάτησε κι ἄρχισαν οἱ ἐλπίδες τῶν γρύλων.

Γι' αὐτὸ λοιπὸν κι ἐσεῖς παλληκάρια μου μὲ τὸ κρασὶ τὰ φιλιὰ καὶ τὰ
φύλλα στὸ στόμα σας
Θέλω νὰ βγεῖτε γυμνοὶ στὰ ποτάμια
Νὰ τραγουδῆστε τὴ Μπαρμπαριὰ ὅπως ὁ ξυλουργὸς κυνηγάει τοὺς
σκίνους

And one lost elephant means always more
      than a girl's breasts dancing
Only in the mountains let the roofs of lonely chapels
      blaze up at the will of the evening star
Let waves of birds break over the rigging of the lemon tree
With the steady white blast of a new way of walking
And then the angels of the wind shall come
      in body like swans which are immaculate, soft, unchanging
Among the steamrollers of the emporia and cyclones of the
                                market gardens
When women's eyes turned to coals
      and the chestnut sellers broke their hearts
When the harvest was over and the hopes of the cricket began.

And because of this I would have you, young men,
To go down naked into the rivers
With wine and kisses and leaves in your mouth
To sing of Barbary
      as the carpenter follows the track of the wood's grain

Ὅπως περνάει ἡ ὄχεντρα μὲς ἀπ᾽ τὰ περιβόλια τῶν κριθαριῶν
Μὲ τὰ περήφανα μάτια της ὀργισμένα
Κι ὅπως οἱ ἀστραπὲς ἁλωνίζουν τὰ νιάτα.

Καὶ μὴ γελᾶς καὶ μὴν κλαῖς καὶ μὴ χαίρεσαι
Μὴ σφίγγεις ἄδικα τὰ παπούτσια σου σὰ νὰ φυτεύεις πλατάνια
Μὴ γίνεσαι ΠΕΠΡΩΜΕΝΟΝ
Γιατὶ δὲν εἶναι ὁ σταυραητὸς ἕνα κλεισμένο συρτάρι
Δὲν εἶναι δάκρυ κορομηλιᾶς οὔτε χαμόγελο νούφαρου
Οὔτε φανέλα περιστεριοῦ καὶ μαντολίνο Σουλτάνου
Οὔτε μεταξωτὴ φορεσιὰ γιὰ τὸ κεφάλι τῆς φάλαινας.
Εἶναι πριόνι θαλασσινὸ ποὺ πετσοκόβει τοὺς γλάρους
Εἶναι προσκέφαλο μαραγκοῦ εἶναι ρολόι ζητιάνου
Εἶναι φωτιὰ σ᾽ ἕνα γύφτικο ποὺ κοροϊδεύει τὶς παπαδιὲς καὶ νανουρίζει
      τὰ κρίνα
Εἶναι τῶν Τούρκων συμπεθεριὸ τῶν Αὐστραλῶν πανηγύρι
Εἶναι λημέρι τῶν Οὕγγρων
Ποὺ τὸ χινόπωρο οἱ φουντουκιὲς πᾶνε κρυφὰ κι ἀνταμώνουνται
Βλέπουν τοὺς φρόνιμους πελαργοὺς νὰ βάφουν μαῦρα τ᾽ αὐγά τους

As the viper moves out from the gardens of the barley
With her proud eyes furious
And as the strokes of the lightning thresh the young.

And do not laugh, do not cry, do not be glad
Do not lace your shoes up wrong as if you were planting a plane tree
Do not become PREDESTINED
Because the golden eagle is not a drawer locked up
It is not the tear of a wild plum
      nor the smile of a water-lily
Nor the vest of a dove nor a sultan's mandolin
Nor a silken hat for the head of a whale
It is the sea's hacksaw cutting gulls in pieces
It is the pillow of a carpenter, is the beggar's watch
Is fire in a forge mocking vicars' wives, and singing lilies to sleep
It is relationship by marriage to the Turks, is a fiesta of Australians
Is a den of thieves in Hungary
Where the hazel trees go secretly to meet in autumn
They see the clever storks painting their eggs black

Καὶ τόνε κλαῖνε κι αὐτὲς

Καῖνε τὰ νυχτικά τους καὶ φοροῦν τὸ μισοφόρι τῆς πάπιας

Στρώνουν ἀστέρια καταγῆς γιὰ νὰ πατήσουν οἱ βασιλιάδες

Μὲ τ' ἀσημένια τους χαϊμαλιὰ μὲ τὴν κορώνα καὶ τὴν πορφύρα

Σκορπᾶνε δεντρολίβανο στὶς βραγιὲς

Γιὰ νὰ περάσουν οἱ ποντικοὶ νὰ πᾶνε σ' ἄλλο κελλάρι

Νὰ μποῦνε σ' ἄλλες ἐκκλησιὲς νὰ φᾶν τὶς Ἅγιες Τράπεζες

Κι οἱ κουκουβάγιες παιδιά μου

Οἱ κουκουβάγιες οὐρλιάζουνε

Κι οἱ πεθαμένες καλογριὲς σηκώνουνται νὰ χορέψουν

Μὲ ντέφια τούμπανα καὶ βιολιὰ μὲ πίπιζες καὶ λαγοῦτα

Μὲ φλάμπουρα καὶ μὲ θυμιατὰ μὲ βότανα καὶ μαγνάδια

Μὲ τῆς ἀρκούδας τὸ βρακὶ στὴν παγωμένη κοιλάδα

Τρῶνε τὰ μανιτάρια τῶν κουναβιῶν

Παίζουν κορώνα-γράμματα τὸ δαχτυλίδι τ' Ἀη-Γιαννιοῦ καὶ τὰ φλουριὰ
    τοῦ Ἀράπη

Περιγελᾶνε τὶς μάγισσες

Κόβουν τὰ γένια ἑνὸς παπᾶ μὲ τοῦ Κολοκοτρώνη τὸ γιαταγάνι

And then they also weep
They put their night-dress on the fire and wear
    the petticoat of a duck
They set down stars on the earth
    for kings to walk on
With silver charms, the crown and the purple
They scatter rosemary on fresh furrows
That the mice may cross over into another cellar
That they may enter other churches to eat altars
And the owls, my friends,
The owls are hooting,
And the dead nuns are rising up to dance
With tambourine and drum and violin,
    with lute and bagpipe
With banner and thurible, herbs and things of magic
With the she-bear's breeches in the frozen valley
They eat the mushrooms of the house martins
They play at heads and tails for St John's ring
    and the black man's gold guineas
They laugh at witches
They cut off a priest's whiskers with the yataghan of Kolokotronis

Λούζονται μὲς στὴν ἄχνη τοῦ λιβανιοῦ
Κι ὕστερα ψέλνοντας ἀργὰ μπαίνουν ξανὰ στὴ γῆ καὶ σωπαίνουν
Ὅπως σωπαίνουν τὰ κύματα ὅπως ὁ κοῦκος τὴ χαραυγὴ ὅπως ὁ λύχνος
    τὸ βράδυ.

Ἔτσι σ' ἕνα πιθάρι βαθὺ τὸ σταφύλι ξεραίνεται καὶ στὸ καμπαναριὸ
    μιᾶς συκιᾶς κιτρινίζει τὸ μῆλο
Ἔτσι μὲ μιὰ γραβάτα φανταχτερὴ
Στὴν τέντα τῆς κληματαριᾶς τὸ καλοκαίρι ἀνασαίνει
Ἔτσι κοιμᾶται ὁλόγυμνη μέσα στὶς ἄσπρες κερασιὲς μιὰ τρυφερή μου
    ἀγάπη
Ἕνα κορίτσι ἀμάραντο σὰ μυγδαλιᾶς κλωνάρι
Μὲ τὸ κεφάλι στὸν ἀγκώνα της γερτὸ καὶ τὴν παλάμη πάνω στὸ
    φλουρί της
Πάνω στὴν πρωινή του θαλπωρὴ ὅταν σιγά-σιγὰ σὰν τὸν κλέφτη
Ἀπὸ τὸ παραθύρι τῆς ἄνοιξης μπαίνει ὁ αὐγερινὸς νὰ τὴν ξυπνήσει!

They wash in the smoke of frankincense
And later, slowly chanting, they go back again into the earth and
                                                    are silent
As the waves are silent, as the cuckoo at dawn, as the lamp at evening.

That is how the grape goes dry deep inside the pot
        and the apple turns yellow in the bell-tower of a fig tree
That is how in a tawdry cravat
The summer is breathing under a tent of vine-leaves
That is how quite naked among white cherry trees my darling sleeps
A girl unwithering as a branch of the almond tree
With her head at rest on the crook of her arm, and her hand on her
                                                    golden coin
On its warmness in the morning,
        when quietly, quietly, like a thief
From the window of the spring
        comes in the morning star that shall awaken her!

Λένε πὼς τρέμουν τὰ βουνὰ καὶ πὼς θυμώνουν τὰ ἔλατα
Ὅταν ἡ νύχτα ροκανάει τὶς πρόκες τῶν κεραμιδιῶν νὰ μποῦν οἱ
    καλικάντζαροι μέσα
Ὅταν ρουφάει ἡ κόλαση τὸν ἀφρισμένο μόχθο τῶν χειμάρρων
Ἢ ὅταν ἡ χωρίστρα τῆς πιπεριᾶς γίνεται τοῦ βοριᾶ κλωτσοσκούφι.

They say the mountains shiver and the fir trees are enraged
When night crunches up the pegs of the roof-tiles for familiars
                                                    to enter in
When the swill of hell runs in the froth and trouble of winter streams
Or when the parted hair of the pepper tree becomes a spinning-top
                                                    for the north wind.

Μόνο τὰ βόδια τῶν Ἀχαιῶν μὲς στὰ παχιὰ λιβάδια τῆς Θεσσαλίας
Βόσκουν ἀκμαῖα καὶ δυνατὰ μὲ τὸν αἰώνιο ἥλιο ποὺ τὰ κοιτάζει
Τρῶνε χορτάρι πράσινο φύλλα τῆς λεύκας σέλινα πίνουνε καθαρὸ νερὸ
     μὲς στ' αὐλάκια
Μυρίζουν τὸν ἱδρῶτα τῆς γῆς κι ὕστερα πέφτουνε βαριὰ κάτω ἀπ' τὸν
     ἴσκιο τῆς ἰτιᾶς νὰ κοιμηθοῦνε.

Πετᾶτε τοὺς νεκροὺς εἶπ' ὁ Ἡράκλειτος κι εἶδε τὸν οὐρανὸ νὰ χλωμιάζει
Κι εἶδε στὴ λάσπη δυὸ μικρὰ κυκλάμινα νὰ φιλιοῦνται
Κι ἔπεσε νὰ φιλήσει κι αὐτὸς τὸ πεθαμένο σῶμα του μὲς στὸ φιλόξενο
     χῶμα
Ὅπως ὁ λύκος κατεβαίνει ἀπ' τοὺς δρυμοὺς νὰ δεῖ τὸ ψόφιο σκυλὶ καὶ
     νὰ κλάψει.
Τί νὰ μοῦ κάμει ἡ σταλαγματιὰ ποὺ λάμπει στὸ μέτωπό σου;
Τὸ ξέρω πάνω στὰ χείλια σου ἔγραψε ὁ κεραυνὸς τ' ὄνομά του
Τὸ ξέρω μέσα στὰ μάτια σου ἔχτισε ἕνας ἀητὸς τὴ φωλιά του
Μὰ ἐδῶ στὴν ὄχτη τὴν ὑγρὴ μόνο ἕνας δρόμος ὑπάρχει
Μόνο ἕνας δρόμος ἀπατηλὸς καὶ πρέπει νὰ τὸν περάσεις
Πρέπει στὸ αἷμα νὰ βουτηχτεῖς πρὶν ὁ καιρὸς σὲ προφτάσει
Καὶ νὰ διαβεῖς ἀντίπερα νὰ ξαναβρεῖς τοὺς συντρόφους σου

Only the cattle of the Achaeans in the fat meadows of Thessaly
Graze thriving and strong in the everlasting sun that watches them
They eat green grass, leaves of poplar, parsley, drink clean water
                                                in the channels
They smell the sweat of the earth and later fall down
        heavily in the shade of the willow and sleep.

Reject the dead, said Heraclitus, and saw the sky turn pale
And saw two little cyclamens kissing in the dirt
And he too lay down to kiss his own dead body on the hospitable earth
As the wolf comes down from the woods to see the dog's carcass
                                                and to weep.
What is it to me, the drop that runs and glitters down your forehead?
I know the lightning has written his name on your lips
I know an eagle has built his nest in your eyes
But here on the wet bank there is only one road
Only one deceiving road and you must take it
You must dive down into blood before occasion overtakes you
And cross to the other side to rediscover your comrades
Flowers birds deer

Ἄνθη πουλιὰ ἐλάφια

Νὰ βρεῖς μιὰν ἄλλη θάλασσα μιὰν ἄλλη ἁπαλοσύνη

Νὰ πιάσεις ἀπὸ τὰ λουριὰ τοῦ Ἀχιλλέα τ' ἄλογα

Ἀντὶ νὰ κάθεσαι βουβὴ τὸν ποταμὸ νὰ μαλώνεις

Τὸν ποταμὸ νὰ λιθοβολεῖς ὅπως ἡ μάνα τοῦ Κίτσου.

Γιατὶ κι ἐσὺ θά 'χεις χαθεῖ κι ἡ ὀμορφιά σου θά 'χει γεράσει.

Μέσα στοὺς κλώνους μιᾶς λυγαριᾶς βλέπω τὸ παιδικό σου πουκάμισο νὰ
     στεγνώνει

Πάρ' το σημαία τῆς ζωῆς νὰ σαβανώσεις τὸ θάνατο

Κι ἂς μὴ λυγίσει ἡ καρδιά σου

Κι ἂς μὴν κυλήσει τὸ δάκρυ σου πάνω στὴν ἀδυσώπητη τούτη γῆ

Ὅπως ἐκύλησε μιὰ φορὰ στὴν παγωμένη ἐρημιὰ τὸ δάκρυ τοῦ πιγκουίνου

Δὲν ὠφελεῖ τὸ παράπονο

Ἴδια παντοῦ θά 'ναι ἡ ζωὴ μὲ τὸ σουραύλι τῶν φιδιῶν στὴ χώρα τῶν
     φαντασμάτων

Μὲ τὸ τραγούδι τῶν ληστῶν στὰ δάση τῶν ἀρωμάτων

Μὲ τὸ μαχαίρι ἑνὸς καημοῦ στὰ μάγουλα τῆς ἐλπίδας

Μὲ τὸ μαράζι μιᾶς ἄνοιξης στὰ φυλλοκάρδια τοῦ γκιώνη

Φτάνει ἕνα ἀλέτρι νὰ βρεθεῖ κι ἕνα δρεπάνι κοφτερὸ σ' ἕνα χαρούμενο χέρι

Φτάνει ν' ἀνθίσει μόνο

Λίγο σιτάρι γιὰ τὶς γιορτὲς λίγο κρασὶ γιὰ τὴ θύμηση λίγο νερὸ γιὰ τὴ
     σκόνη...

To find another sea, another gentleness,
To seize the horses of Achilles by the reins
Instead of sitting dumb to quarrel with the river
To throw stones at the river like the mother of Kitsos.
Because you in your turn will have been ruined and your beauty
will have grown old.
On the branches of a willow I see the shirt of your childhood
hanging up to dry
Take the flag of life for a sheet to wind up death
And let your heart not bend
And let your tear not fall on this unrelenting earth
As the penguin's tear once fell in the frozen desert
Lamentation is useless
Everywhere life will be the same, with the flute of the serpents in the
country of ghosts
With the song of the robbers in the spice groves
With the knife of a sorrow in the cheek of hope
With the grief of a springtime nestling in the heart of the young owl
It is enough if a plough is found and a sickle sharp in a happy hand
Enough if there should flower only
A little grain for festivals, a little wine for remembrance, a little
water for the dust…

Στοῦ πικραμένου τὴν αὐλὴ ἥλιος δὲν ἀνατέλλει
Μόνο σκουλήκια βγαίνουνε νὰ κοροϊδέψουν τ᾽ ἄστρα
Μόνο φυτρώνουν ἄλογα στὶς μυρμηγκοφωλιὲς
Καὶ νυχτερίδες τρῶν πουλιὰ καὶ κατουρᾶνε σπέρμα.

In the backyard of the embittered no sun rises
Only worms come out to deride the stars
Only horses are in bud on ant-hills
And bats are eating birds and pissing seed.

Στοῦ πικραμένου τὴν αὐλὴ δὲ βασιλεύει ἡ νύχτα
Μόνο ξερνᾶν οἱ φυλλωσιὲς ἕνα ποτάμι δάκρυα
Ὅταν περνάει ὁ διάβολος νὰ καβαλήσει τὰ σκυλιὰ
Καὶ τὰ κοράκια κολυμπᾶν σ' ἕνα πηγάδι μ' αἷμα.

Στοῦ πικραμένου τὴν αὐλὴ τὸ μάτι ἔχει στερέψει
Ἔχει παγώσει τὸ μυαλὸ κι ἔχει ἡ καρδιὰ πετρώσει
Κρέμονται σάρκες βατραχιῶν στὰ δόντια τῆς ἀράχνης
Σκούζουν ἀκρίδες νηστικὲς σὲ βρυκολάκων πόδια.

Στοῦ πικραμένου τὴν αὐλὴ βγαίνει χορτάρι μαῦρο
Μόνο ἕνα βράδυ τοῦ Μαγιοῦ πέρασε ἕνας ἀγέρας
Ἕνα περπάτημα ἐλαφρὺ σὰ σκίρτημα τοῦ κάμπου
Ἕνα φιλὶ τῆς θάλασσας τῆς ἀφροστολισμένης.

In the backyard of the embittered night is king
Only the throngs of leaves throw out a river of tears
When the devil goes by to ride on the backs of dogs
And the crows are diving in a well of blood.

In the backyard of the embittered the eye has run dry
The brain has turned to ice and the heart petrified
Frogs' flesh hangs from the teeth of the spider
Crickets howl starving at the feet of vampires.

In the backyard of the embittered grass comes up black
Only, one May evening, a breeze went by
A light footstep like the movement of a meadow
A kiss of the foam-embroidered sea.

Κι ἂν θὰ διψάσεις γιὰ νερὸ θὰ στίψουμε ἕνα σύννεφο
Κι ἂν θὰ πεινάσεις γιὰ ψωμὶ θὰ σφάξουμε ἕνα ἀηδόνι
Μόνο καρτέρει μιὰ στιγμὴ ν' ἀνοίξει ὁ πικραπήγανος
Ν' ἀστράψει ὁ μαῦρος οὐρανὸς νὰ λουλουδίσει ὁ φλόμος.

Μὰ εἶταν ἀγέρας κι ἔφυγε κορυδαλλὸς κι ἐχάθη
Εἶταν τοῦ Μάη τὸ πρόσωπο τοῦ φεγγαριοῦ ἡ ἀσπράδα
Ἕνα περπάτημα ἐλαφρὺ σὰ σκίρτημα τοῦ κάμπου
Ἕνα φιλὶ τῆς θάλασσας τῆς ἀφροστολισμένης.

And if you are thirsty for water we shall milk a cloud
And if you are hungry for bread we shall slaughter a nightingale
Only hold out a moment for the bitter herb to open
For the dark heavens to flash, for the candlewick to blossom.

But it was a wind that went, a lark that perished
It was the face of May, the whiteness of the moon
A light footstep like the movement of a meadow
A kiss of the foam-embroidered sea.

Ξύπνησε γάργαρο νερὸ ἀπὸ τὴ ρίζα τοῦ πεύκου νὰ βρεῖς τὰ μάτια τῶν σπουργιτιῶν καὶ νὰ τὰ ζωντανέψεις ποτίζοντας τὸ χῶμα μὲ μυρωδιὰ βασιλικοῦ καὶ μὲ σφυρίγματα σαύρας. Τὸ ξέρω εἶσαι μιὰ φλέβα γυμνὴ κάτω ἀπὸ τὸ φοβερὸ βλέμμα τοῦ ἄνεμου εἶσαι μιὰ σπίθα βουβὴ μέσα στὸ λαμπερὸ πλῆθος τῶν ἄστρων. Δὲ σὲ προσέχει κανεὶς κανεὶς δὲ σταματᾶ ν' ἀκούσει τὴν ἀνάσα σου μὰ σὺ μὲ τὸ βαρύ σου περπάτημα μὲς στὴν ἀγέρωχη φύση θὰ φτάσεις μιὰ μέρα στὰ φύλλα τῆς βερυκοκιᾶς θ' ἀνέβεις στὰ λυγερὰ κορμιὰ τῶν μικρῶν σπάρτων καὶ θὰ

Wake gargling water out of the root of the pine and discover the eyes of the sparrows and enliven them sprinkling the earth with a smell of basil and the whistles of the lizard. I know you are a bare vein under the frightful stare of the wind a deaf spark among the glistening multitude of stars. No one observes you no one stops to listen to your breathing but you in your heavy pacing through the pride of nature shall come one day to the leaves of the apricot tree shall climb into the bending bodies of the little shrubs and shall roll

κυλήσεις ἀπὸ τὰ μάτια μιᾶς ἀγαπητικιᾶς σὰν ἐφηβικὸ φεγγάρι. Ὑπάρχει μιὰ πέτρα ἀθάνατη ποὺ κάποτε περαστικὸς ἕνας ἀνθρώπινος ἄγγελος ἔγραψε τ' ὄνομά του ἐπάνω της κι ἕνα τραγούδι ποὺ δὲν τὸ ξέρει ἀκόμα κανεὶς οὔτε τὰ πιὸ τρελὰ παιδιὰ οὔτε τὰ πιὸ σοφὰ τ' ἀηδόνια. Εἶναι κλεισμένη τώρα σὲ μιὰ σπηλιὰ τοῦ βουνοῦ Ντέβι μέσα στὶς λαγκαδιὲς καὶ στὰ φαράγγια τῆς πατρικῆς μου γῆς μὰ ὅταν ἀνοίξει κάποτε καὶ τιναχτεῖ ἐνάντια στὴ φθορὰ καὶ στὸ χρόνο αὐτὸ τὸ ἀγγελικὸ τραγούδι θὰ πάψει ξαφνικὰ ἡ βροχὴ καὶ θὰ στεγνώσουν οἱ λάσπες τὰ χιόνια θὰ λιώσουν στὰ βουνὰ θὰ κελαηδήσει ὁ ἄνεμος τὰ χελιδόνια θ' ἀναστηθοῦν οἱ λυγαριὲς θὰ ριγήσουν κι οἱ ἄνθρωποι μὲ τὰ κρύα μάτια καὶ τὰ χλωμὰ πρόσωπα ὅταν ἀκούσουν τὶς καμπάνες νὰ χτυπᾶν μέσα στὰ ραγισμένα καμπαναριὰ μοναχές τους θὰ βροῦν καπέλα γιορτινὰ νὰ φορέσουν καὶ φιόγκους φανταχτερούς νὰ δέσουν στὰ παπούτσια τους. Γιατὶ τότε κανεὶς δὲ θ' ἀστειεύεται πιὰ τὸ αἷμα τῶν ρυακιῶν θὰ ξεχειλίσει τὰ ζῶα θὰ κόψουν τὰ χαλινάρια τους στὰ παχνιὰ τὸ χόρτο θὰ πρασινίσει στοὺς στάβλους στὰ κεραμίδια θὰ πεταχτοῦν ὁλόχλωρες παπαροῦνες καὶ μάηδες καὶ σ' ὅλα τὰ σταυροδρόμια θ' ἀνάψουν κόκκινες φωτιὲς τὰ μεσάνυχτα. Τότε θὰ 'ρθοῦν σιγὰ-σιγὰ τὰ φοβισμένα κορίτσια γιὰ νὰ πετάξουν τὸ τελευταῖο τους ροῦχο στὴ φωτιὰ κι ὁλόγυμνα θὰ χορέψουν τριγύρω της ὅπως τὴν ἐποχὴ ἀκριβῶς ποὺ εἴμαστον κι ἐμεῖς νέοι κι ἄνοιγε ἕνα παράθυρο τὴν

down from the eyes of a beloved like an adolescent moon. There is an immortal stone where once in passing a human angel wrote his name on it and a song no one knows yet not the maddest boys not the wisest nightingales. It is locked up now in a cave on Mount Devi among the valleys and the ravines of my own country but when that opens up one day and the angelic song leaps out against decay and time the rain will suddenly cease and the muddy places will be dried the snow will melt on the mountains wind will be loud swallows shall be resurrected willow trees shall shiver and men with cold eyes and pale faces when they shall hear the bells ring on their own in the cracked belfries shall find holiday hats to wear and fantastical decorations to tie up their shoes. Because then no one will be joking any more the blood in the brooks will overflow the animals will break their bridles in the stall hay will turn green in stables poppies and mayflowers sprout fresh out of the roof-tiles and at every crossroads girls will come to throw the last of their clothes into the fire and they will dance around it quite naked just like the days when we were young too and a window opened at dawn to plant a carnation blazing in the breast. My friends perhaps the memory of forefathers may be a deeper consolation and a more honourable company than a handful of rose-scented water and the intoxication of beauty nothing other than

αὐγὴ γιὰ νὰ φυτρώσει στὸ στῆθος τους ἕνα φλογάτο γαρύφαλο. Παιδιὰ ἴσως ἡ μνήμη τῶν προγόνων νὰ εἶναι βαθύτερη παρηγοριὰ καὶ πιὸ πολύτιμη συντροφιὰ ἀπὸ μιὰ χούφτα ροδόσταμο καὶ τὸ μεθύσι τῆς ὀμορφιᾶς τίποτε διαφορετικὸ ἀπὸ τὴν κοιμισμένη τριανταφυλλιὰ τοῦ Εὐρώτα. Καληνύχτα λοιπὸν βλέπω σωροὺς πεφτάστερα νὰ σᾶς λικνίζουν τὰ ὄνειρα μὰ ἐγὼ κρατῶ στὰ δάχτυλά μου τὴ μουσικὴ γιὰ μιὰ καλύτερη μέρα. Οἱ ταξιδιῶτες τῶν Ἰνδιῶν ξέρουνε περισσότερα νὰ σᾶς ποῦν ἀπ᾿ τοὺς Βυζαντινοὺς χρονογράφους.

the sleeping rose of the Eurotas. Goodnight then I see crowds of falling stars rocking your dreams but I am holding in my fingers the music for a better day. Travellers from the Indies have more to tell you than Byzantine chroniclers.

Ο ἄνθρωπος κατὰ τὸν ροῦν τῆς μυστηριώδους ζωῆς του
Κατέλιπεν εἰς τοὺς ἀπογόνους του δείγματα πολλαπλᾶ καὶ ἀντάξια τῆς
  ἀθανάτου καταγωγῆς του
Ὅπως ἐπίσης κατέλιπεν ἴχνη τῶν ἐρειπίων τοῦ λυκαυγοῦς χιονοστιβάδας
  οὐρανίων ἑρπετῶν χαρταετοὺς ἀδάμαντας καὶ βλέμματα
  ὑακίνθων
Ἐν μέσῳ ἀναστεναγμῶν δακρύων πείνης οἰμωγῶν καὶ τέφρας ὑπογείων
  φρεάτων.

Man in the stream of his mysterious life
Has left to his descendants patterns various and worthy of his
immortal origin
As he has also left traces of the ruins of daybreak,
snowdrifts of heavenly reptiles, paper eagles, diamonds and
the glances of hyacinths
In the midst of sighs, of tears, of hunger, of lamentations
and of the ash of wells under the earth.

Πόσο πολὺ σὲ ἀγάπησα ἐγὼ μονάχα τὸ ξέρω
Ἐγὼ ποὺ κάποτε σ' ἄγγιξα μὲ τὰ μάτια τῆς πούλιας
Καὶ μὲ τὴ χαίτη τοῦ φεγγαριοῦ σ' ἀγκάλιασα καὶ χορέψαμε μὲς στοὺς
    καλοκαιριάτικους κάμπους
Πάνω στὴ θερισμένη καλαμιὰ καὶ φάγαμε μαζὶ τὸ κομένο τριφύλλι
Μαύρη μεγάλη θάλασσα μὲ τόσα βότσαλα τριγύρω στὸ λαιμὸ τόσα
    χρωματιστὰ πετράδια στὰ μαλλιά σου.

How much I have loved you I alone know
I who touched you once with the eyes of the Pleiades
And embraced you in the wild hair of the moon and we danced in
                                        the summer fields
On the stubble after harvest, and we ate the cut clover
Dark and great sea with so many pebbles round your neck, so
    many coloured stones in your hair.

Ἕνα καράβι μπαίνει στὸ γιαλὸ ἕνα μαγγανοπήγαδο σκουριασμένο
    βογγάει
Μιὰ τούφα γαλανὸς καπνὸς μὲς στὸ τριανταφυλλὶ τοῦ ὁρίζοντα
Ἴδιος μὲ τὴ φτερούγα τοῦ γερανοῦ ποὺ σπαράζει
Στρατιὲς χελιδονιῶν περιμένουνε νὰ ποῦν στοὺς ἀντρειωμένους τὸ
    καλωσόρισες
Μπράτσα σηκώνουνται γυμνὰ μὲ χαραγμένες ἄγκυρες στὴ μασχάλη
Μπερδεύουνται κραυγὲς παιδιῶν μὲ τὸ κελάδημα τοῦ πουνέντε
Μέλισσες μπαινοβγαίνουνε μὲς στὰ ρουθούνια τῶν ἀγελάδων
Μαντήλια καλαματιανὰ κυματίζουνε
Καὶ μιὰ καμπάνα μακρινὴ βάφει τὸν οὐρανὸ μὲ λουλάκι
Σὰν τὴ φωνὴ κάποιου σήμαντρου ποὺ ταξιδεύει μέσα στ' ἀστέρια
Τόσους αἰῶνες φευγάτο
Ἀπὸ τῶν Γότθων τὴν ψυχὴ κι ἀπὸ τοὺς τρούλλους τῆς Βαλτιμόρης
Κι ἀπ' τὴ χαμένη Ἁγιὰ-Σοφιὰ τὸ μέγα μοναστήρι.
Μὰ πάνω στ' ἀψηλὰ βουνὰ ποιοὶ νὰ 'ναι αὐτοὶ ποὺ κοιτᾶνε
Μὲ τὴν ἀκύμαντη ματιὰ καὶ τὸ γαλήνιο πρόσωπο;
Ποιᾶς πυρκαγιᾶς νὰ 'ναι ἀντίλαλος αὐτὸς ὁ κουρνιαχτὸς στὸν ἀγέρα;
Μήνα ὁ Καλύβας πολεμάει μήνα ὁ Λεβεντογιάννης;
Μήπως ἀμάχη ἐπιάσανεν οἱ Γερμανοὶ μὲ τοὺς Μανιάτες;
Οὐδ' ὁ Καλύβας πολεμάει κι οὐδ' ὁ Λεβεντογιάννης

A ship goes out to sea, a rusted water-wheel is groaning
A tuft of blue smoke inside the rose of the horizon
It is the wing-beat of the crane
Armies of swallows are waiting to welcome in the brave
Bare arms rise up, with anchors cut on their shoulders
The cries of children tangle in the loud noise of the west wind
Bees move in and out of the nostrils of the cattle
Scarves of Kalamáta silk are streaming
And a faraway bell is painting heaven indigo
Like the voice of some monastic summons journeying among
                                                    the stars
So many ages a refugee
From the soul of the Goths and the domes of Baltimore
And from lost Hagia Sophia, that great abbey.
But who are these, watching on the heights of the mountains
With steady eyes and peace in their faces?
To what conflagration does this dust-cloud on the wind answer?
Can it be Kalybas is fighting now, or is it Leventoyannis?
Have the Germans gone to war against the Mani?
Kalybas is not fighting now, nor is Leventoyannis

Οὔτε κι ἀμάχη ἐπιάσανεν οἱ Γερμανοὶ μὲ τοὺς Μανιάτες.

Πύργοι φυλᾶνε σιωπηλοὶ μιὰ στοιχειωμένη πριγκίπισσα

Κορφὲς κυπαρισσιῶν συντροφεύουνε μιὰ πεθαμένη ἀνεμώνη

Τσοπαναρέοι ἀτάραχοι μ' ἕνα καλάμι φλαμουριᾶς λένε τὸ πρωινό τους
τραγούδι

Ἕνας ἀνόητος κυνηγὸς ρίχνει μιὰ ντουφεκιὰ στὰ τρυγόνια

Κι ἕνας παλιὸς ἀνεμόμυλος λησμονημένος ἀπ' ὅλους

Μὲ μιὰ βελόνα δελφινιοῦ ράβει τὰ σάπια του πανιὰ μοναχός του

Καὶ κατεβαίνει ἀπ' τὶς πλαγιὲς μὲ τὸν καράγιαλη πρίμα

Ὅπως κατέβαινε ὁ Ἄδωνις στὰ μονοπάτια τοῦ Χελμοῦ νὰ πεῖ μιὰ
καλησπέρα τῆς Γκόλφως.

Χρόνια καὶ χρόνια πάλεψα μὲ τὸ μελάνι καὶ τὸ σφυρὶ βασανισμένη
καρδιά μου

Μὲ τὸ χρυσάφι καὶ τὴ φωτιὰ γιὰ νὰ σοῦ κάμω ἕνα κέντημα

Ἕνα ζουμπούλι πορτοκαλιᾶς

Μιὰν ἀνθισμένη κυδωνιὰ νὰ σὲ παρηγορήσω

Ἐγὼ ποὺ κάποτε σ' ἄγγιξα μὲ τὰ μάτια τῆς πούλιας

Καὶ μὲ τὴ χαίτη τοῦ φεγγαριοῦ σ' ἀγκάλιασα καὶ χορέψαμε μὲς στοὺς
καλοκαιριάτικους κάμπους

And the Germans have not gone to war against the Mani.

Silent towers are guarding the ghost of a princess

The tops of cypresses keep company with a dead anemone

Untroubled shepherds play their morning song on a pipe
                                                    of lime-wood

A stupid huntsman fires off his gun at the doves

And an old windmill forgotten by everyone

Patches his rotted sails, alone, with a needle of dolphin's bone

And descends from the heights with the north-west wind behind him

Just as Adonis descended by the footpaths of Chelmos to say good
                                        evening to his shepherdess.

For years and years I have struggled with ink and hammer, my
                                                    tormented heart,

With gold and with fire to make you an embroidery

A hyacinth from the orange tree,

A quince tree in flower to comfort you

I who touched you once with the eyes of the Pleiades

And embraced you in the wild hair of the moon and we danced in
                                                    the summer fields

Πάνω στὴ θερισμένη καλαμιὰ καὶ φάγαμε μαζί τὸ κομένο τριφύλλι
Μαύρη μεγάλη μοναξιὰ μὲ τόσα βότσαλα τριγύρω στὸ λαιμὸ τόσα
χρωματιστὰ πετράδια στὰ μαλλιά σου.

On the stubble after harvest, and we ate the cut clover
Dark and great loneliness with so many pebbles round your neck,
    so many coloured stones in your hair.

Some modern Greek poetry

Odysseus Elytis
SELECTED POEMS
Translated by Edmund Keeley and Philip Sherrard

Odysseus Elytis
THE AXION ESTI
Translated by Edmund Keeley and George Savidis

George Pavlopoulos
THE CELLAR
Translated by Peter Levi

Yannis Ritsos
THE FOURTH DIMENSION
Translated by Peter Green and Beverly Bardsley

George Seferis
COMPLETE POEMS
Translated by Edmund Keeley and Philip Sherrard

Poetry by Peter Levi and Sally Purcell

Peter Levi

COLLECTED POEMS
1955–1975

FIVE AGES

GOODBYE TO THE ART OF POETRY

SHADOW AND BONE

THE RAGS OF TIME

REED MUSIC

VIRIDITAS

Sally Purcell

THE HOLLY QUEEN

DARK OF DAY

FOSSIL UNICORN

COLLECTED POEMS